Keto Cookbook for Beginners

Quick and Easy Ketogenic Recipes to Boost Your Metabolism and Stay Healthy

Yasmine Morris

Table of Contents

BREAKFAST 8

1. TURMERIC CHICKEN AND KALE SALAD WITH LEMON AND HONEY 8
2. BUCKWHEAT SPAGHETTI WITH CHICKEN CABBAGE 12
3. ASIAN KING JUMPED JAMP 16
4. BUCKWHEAT SALAD 19
5. GREEK SALAD SKEWERS 21
6. KALE, EDAMAME AND TOFU CURRY 23

LUNCH 27

7. BLACK BEAN AND SWEET POTATO HASH 27
8. VEGAN SALMON BAGEL 29
9. KETO HOT BUFFALO WINGS 31
10. TROUT AND CHILI NUTS 34
11. BACON AND EGG QUESADILLAS 36
12. CHICKEN THIGHS WITH VEGETABLES 39
13. CHICKEN DIPPED IN TOMATILLO SAUCE 41
14. CHICKEN WITH LEMON PARSLEY BUTTER 43
15. KETO PAPRIKA CHICKEN 45

DINNER...47

16. **Black Bean Salsa** 47
17. **Mung Sprouts Salsa**...49
18. **Sprouts and Apples Snack Salad** 51
19. **Dijon Celery Salad** 53
20. **Napa Cabbage Slaw**..55

VEGETABLES 57

21. **Jalapeno and Cheese Egg Muffins** 57
22. **Cheesy Tomato and Olive Muffins**...........................60
23. **Pumpkin Bread**...62
24. **Buttery Broccoli and Bacon** 64
25. **Broccoli Salad with Bacon**..66
26. **Roasted Green Beans** 68

MEAT...71

27. **Beef, Pepper and Green Beans Stir-fry**...................71
28. **Cheesy Meatloaf**..74

POULTRY AND EGGS..77

29. **Chili Chicken Kabobs with Tahini** 77
30. **Chicken with Eggplant & Tomatoes** 80

SEAFOOD 83

31. **CHEESY GARLIC BREAD WITH SALMON** 83

32. **SALMON PASTA SALAD** 86

SNACKS.. 89

33. **NDS** 89

34. **GREEN TABASCO DEVILLED EGGS** 91

SALADS.. 93

35. **SEARED SQUID SALAD WITH RED CHILI DRESSING** 93

SOUPS AND STEWS 97

36. **SAUSAGE SOUP WITH TOMATOES & ZUCCHINI NOODLES**.......97

37. **SHIRATAKI SOUP**...100

DESSERTS 103

38. **HEART CHOCOLATES** 103

39. **CARAMEL CANDIES (2ND VERSION)**..............................105

40. **TOFFEES WITH MOCHA** 107

BREAKFAST

1. Turmeric Chicken and Kale Salad with Lemon and Honey

Preparation Time: 20 minutes

Cooking Time: 15 minutes

Servings: 4

Ingredients:

- For the chicken:
- 1 teaspoon of clarified butter or 1 tablespoon of coconut oil
- ½ medium brown onion, diced
- 250-300 g / 9 ounces minced chicken meat or diced chicken legs

- 1 large garlic clove, diced
- 1 teaspoon of turmeric powder
- 1 teaspoon of lime zest
- ½ lime juice
- ½ teaspoon of salt + pepper
- For the salad:
- 6 stalks of broccoli or 2 cups of broccoli flowers
- 2 tablespoons of pumpkin seeds (seeds)
- 3 large cabbage leaves, stems removed and chopped
- ½ sliced avocado
- Handful of fresh coriander leaves, chopped
- Handful of fresh parsley leaves, chopped
- For the dressing:
- 3 tablespoons of lime juice
- 1 small garlic clove, diced or grated

- 3 tablespoons of virgin olive oil (I used 1 tablespoon of avocado oil and 2 tablespoons of EVO)
- 1 teaspoon of raw honey
- ½ teaspoon whole or Dijon mustard
- ½ teaspoon of sea salt with pepper

Directions:

1. Heat the coconut oil in a pan. Add the onion and sauté over medium heat for 4-5 minutes, until golden brown. Add the minced chicken and garlic and stir 2-3 minutes over medium-high heat, separating.
2. Add your turmeric, lime zest, lime juice, salt and pepper, and cook, stirring consistently, for another 3-4 minutes. Set the ground beef aside.
3. While your chicken is cooking, put a small saucepan of water to the boil. Add your broccoli and cook for 2

minutes. Rinse with cold water and cut into 3-4 pieces each.

4. Add the pumpkin seeds to the chicken pan and toast over medium heat for 2 minutes, frequently stirring to avoid burning. Season with a little salt. Set aside. Raw pumpkin seeds are also good to use.
5. Put the chopped cabbage in a salad bowl and pour it over the dressing. Using your hands, mix, and massage the cabbage with the dressing. This will soften the cabbage, a bit like citrus juice with fish or beef Carpaccio: it "cooks" it a little.
6. Finally, mix the cooked chicken, broccoli, fresh herbs, pumpkin seeds, and avocado slices.

Nutrition: 232 calories Fat 11 Fiber 9 Carbs 8 Protein 14

2. Buckwheat Spaghetti with Chicken Cabbage

Preparation Time: 15 minutes

Cooking Time: 15 minutes'

Servings: 2

Ingredients:

- For the noodles:
- 2-3 handfuls of cabbage leaves (removed from the stem and cut)
- Buckwheat noodles 150g / 5oz (100% buckwheat, without wheat)
- 3-4 shiitake mushrooms, sliced
- 1 teaspoon of coconut oil or butter
- 1 brown onion, finely chopped

- 1 medium chicken breast, sliced or diced
- 1 long red pepper, thinly sliced (seeds in or out depending on how hot you like it)
- 2 large garlic cloves, diced
- 2-3 tablespoons of Tamari sauce (gluten-free soy sauce)
- For the miso dressing:
- 1 tablespoon and a half of fresh organic miso
- 1 tablespoon of Tamari sauce
- 1 tablespoon of extra virgin olive oil
- 1 tablespoon of lemon or lime juice
- 1 teaspoon of sesame oil (optional)

Directions:

1. Boil a medium saucepan of water. Add the black cabbage and cook 1 minute, until it is wilted. Remove and reserve, but reserve the water and return to boiling. Add

your soba noodles and cook according to the directions on the package (usually about 5 minutes). Rinse with cold water and reserve.

2. In the meantime, fry the shiitake mushrooms in a little butter or coconut oil (about a teaspoon) for 2-3 minutes, until its color is lightly browned on each side. Sprinkle with sea salt and reserve.
3. In that same pan, heat more coconut oil or lard over medium-high heat. Fry the onion and chili for 2-3 minutes, and then add the chicken pieces. Cook 5 minutes on medium heat, stirring a few times, then add the garlic, tamari sauce, and a little water. Cook for another 2-3 minutes, stirring continuously until your chicken is cooked.
4. Finally, add the cabbage and soba noodles and stir the chicken to warm it.

5. Stir the miso sauce and sprinkle the noodles at the end of the cooking, in this way you will keep alive all the beneficial probiotics in the miso.

Nutrition: 305 calories Fat 11 Fiber 7 Carbs 9 Protein 12

3. Asian King Jumped Jamp

Preparation Time: 15 minutes

Cooking Time: 15 minutes

Servings: 4

Ingredients:

- 150 g / 5 oz. of raw shelled prawns, not chopped
- Two teaspoons of tamari (you can use soy sauce if you don't avoid gluten)
- Two teaspoons of extra virgin olive oil
- 75 g / 2.6 oz. soba (buckwheat pasta)
- 1 garlic clove, finely chopped
- 1 bird's eye chili, finely chopped
- 1 teaspoon finely chopped fresh ginger.
- 20 g / 0.7 oz. of sliced red onions

- 40 g / 1.4 oz. of celery, cut and sliced
- 75 g / 2.6 oz. of chopped green beans
- 50 g / 1.7 oz. of chopped cabbage
- 100 ml / ½ cup of chicken broth
- 5 g celery or celery leaves

Directions:

1. Heat a pan over high heat, and then cook the prawns in 1 teaspoon of tamari and 1 teaspoon of oil for 2-3 minutes. Transfer the prawns to a plate. Clean the pan with kitchen paper as it will be reused.
2. Cook your noodles in boiling water for 5-8 minutes or as indicated on the package. Drain and set aside.
3. Meanwhile, fry the garlic, chili and ginger, red onion, celery, beans, and cabbage in the remaining oil over medium-high heat for 2-3 minutes. Add your broth and

allow it to boil, and then simmer for a minute or two, until the vegetables are cooked but crunchy.

4. Add shrimp, noodles and celery/celery leaves to the pan, bring to a boil again, then remove from the heat and serve.

Nutrition: Calories 213 Protein 34 Fat 2 Carbs 6

4. Buckwheat Salad

Preparation Time: 10 minutes

Cooking Time: 30 minutes

Servings: 4

Ingredients:

- 50 g / 1.7 oz. buckwheat pasta
- Large handful of rockets
- A small handful of basil leaves
- Eight cherry tomatoes halved
- 1/2 avocado, diced
- Ten olives 1 tablespoon. extra olive virgin oil
- 20 g / 0.70 oz. pine nuts

Directions:

1. Combine all the ingredients except your pine nuts.

Arrange your combination on a plate, and then scatter the pine nuts over the top.

Nutrition: 126 calories Fat 6 Fiber 5 Carbs 10 Protein 11

5. Greek Salad Skewers

Preparation Time: 30 minutes

Cooking Time: 0 minutes

Servings: 2

Ingredients:

- Two wooden skewers, soaked in water for 30 minutes before use Eight large black olives
- Eight cherry tomatoes
- 1 yellow pepper, cut into eight squares.
- ½ red onions, you can cut in half and separated into eight pieces
- 100 g / 3.5 oz. (about 10cm) cucumber, cut into four slices and halved
- 100 g / 3.5 oz. feta, cut into eight cubes

- For the dressing:
- 1 tablespoon. extra olive virgin oil
- Juice of ½ lemons
- 1 teaspoon. of your balsamic vinegar
- ½ clove garlic, ensure it peeled and crushed
- Basil leaves chopped (or ½ teaspoon. dried mixed herbs to replace basil and oregano)
- Oregano leaves,
- Salt and grounded black pepper

Directions:

1. Blend each skewer with the salad ingredients in the order

Put all your dressing ingredients into a bowl and mix thoroughly. Pour over the skewers.

Nutrition: Calories 98 Protein 34 Fat 4 Carbs 5

6. Kale, Edamame and Tofu Curry

Preparation Time: 20 minutes

Cooking Time: 40 minutes

Servings: 2

Ingredients:

- 1 tablespoon rapeseed oil
- 1 large onion, chopped
- Four cloves garlic, peeled and grated
- 1 large thumb (7cm) fresh ginger, peeled and grated
- 1 red chili, deseeded and thinly sliced
- 1/2 teaspoon ground turmeric
- 1/4 teaspoon cayenne pepper
- 1 teaspoon paprika
- 1/2 teaspoon ground cumin

- 1 teaspoon salt
- 250 g / 9 oz. dried red lentils
- 1-liter boiling water
- 50 g / 1.7 oz. frozen soya beans
- 200 g / 7 oz. firm tofu, chopped into cubes
- Two tomatoes, roughly chopped
- Juice of 1 lime
- 200 g / 7 oz. kale leaves stalk removed and torn

Directions:

1. Put the oil in a pan over low heat. Add your onion and cook for 5 minutes before adding the garlic, ginger, and chili and cooking for a further 2 minutes. Add your turmeric, cayenne, paprika, cumin, and salt and Stir through before adding the red lentils and stirring again.

2. Pour in the boiling water and allow it to simmer for 10 minutes, reduce the heat and cook for about 20-30 minutes until the curry has a thick '•porridge' consistency.
3. Add your tomatoes, tofu and soya beans and cook for a further 5 minutes. Add your kale leaves and lime juice and cook until the kale is just tender.

Nutrition: Calories 133 Carbohydrate 54 Protein 43

LUNCH

7. Black Bean and Sweet Potato Hash

Preparation Time: 10 minutes

Cooking Time: 30 minutes

Servings: 4 servings

Ingredients:

- 1 cup onion (chopped)
- 1/3 Cup vegetable broth
- 2 garlic (minced)
- 1 cup cooked black beans

- 2 teaspoons hot chili powder
- 2 cups chopped sweet potatoes

Directions:

1. Put the onions in a saucepan over medium heat and add the seasoning and mix.
2. Add potatoes and chili flakes, then mix.
3. Cook for around 12 minutes more until the vegetables are cooked thoroughly.
4. Add the green onion, beans, and salt
5. Cook for more 2 minutes and serve.

Nutrition:

Calories: 239 Fat: 1.1g

Carbohydrates: 71.5g

Protein: 7.8g

8. Vegan Salmon Bagel

Preparation Time: 10 minutes

Cooking Time: 30 minutes

Servings: 2 servings

Ingredients:

- 4 cups of water
- 11/2 red onion
- Vegan cream cheese
- Salt, pepper
- 4 bagels
- 11/2 cup of apple cider vinegar
- 7 carrots

Directions:

1. Preheat to 200 degree Celsius.

2. Slice the carrots.
3. In a mixer to mix, combine sugar, vinegar, and ground pepper.
4. Put the carrot strips in a stir fry bowl, apply the marinade and stir.
5. Cover the carrots with foil and bake for twenty minutes, then switch heat down to 210°F and cook for 40 minutes more.

Nutrition:

Calories: 232

Fat: 9.2g

Carbohydrates: 71.5g

Protein: 7.8g

9. Keto Hot Buffalo wings

Preparation Time: 10 minutes

Cooking Time: 47 minutes

Servings: 3

Ingredients:

- Hot sauce ¼ cup
- Coconut oil 4 tablespoons, plus more for rubbing on the wings
- Chicken wings 12 (fresh or frozen)
- Garlic 1 clove, minced
- Salt ¼ teaspoon
- Paprika ¼ teaspoon
- Cayenne pepper ¼ teaspoon
- Ground black pepper 1 dash

Directions:

1. Preheat your oven to 400 degrees F (200 degrees C).
2. Evenly spread chicken wings on a wire rack placed on a baking dish (it will save wings to become soggy on the bottom).
3. Rub each chicken wing with olive oil and season with salt and pepper, then bake for 45 minutes, or until crispy.
4. Meanwhile, in a saucepan combine coconut oil and garlic and cook over medium heat for 1 minute, or until fragrant.
5. Remove from heat and stir in hot sauce, salt, paprika, cayenne pepper and black pepper.
6. Remove wings from the oven and transfer to a large bowl.

7. Pour hot sauce mixture over wings and toss until each wing is coated with the sauce.
8. Serve immediately.

Nutrition:

Calories: 391

Carbohydrates: 1 g

Fats: 33 g

Protein: 31 g

10. Trout and Chili Nuts

Preparation Time: 10 minutes

Cooking time: 0 minutes

Servings: 2

Ingredients:

- 1.5kg of rainbow trout
- 300gr shelled walnuts
- 1 bunch of parsley
- 9 cloves of garlic
- 7 tablespoons of olive oil
- 2 fresh hot peppers
- The juice of 2 lemons Halls

Directions:

1. Clean and dry the trout then place them in a baking tray.

2. Chop the walnuts, parsley and chili peppers then mash the garlic cloves.
3. Mix the ingredients by adding olive oil, lemon juice and a pinch of salt.
4. Stuff the trout with some of the sauce and use the rest to cover the fish.
5. Bake at 180° for 30/40 minutes.
6. Serve the trout hot or cold.

Nutrition:

Calories 226

Fat 5

Fiber 2

Carbs 7

Protein 9

11. Bacon and Egg Quesadillas

Preparation Time: 10 minutes

Cooking time: 30 minutes

Servings: 3

Ingredients:

- 8 low carb tortilla shells
- 6 eggs
- 1 cup water
- 3 tablespoon butter
- 1 ½ cups grated cheddar cheese
- 1 ½ cups grated Swiss cheese
- 4 bacon slices
- 1 medium onion, thinly sliced
- 1 tablespoon chopped parsley

Directions

1. Bring the eggs to a boil in water over medium heat for 10 minutes. Transfer the eggs to an ice water bath, peel the shells, and chop them; set aside.
2. Meanwhile, as the eggs cook, fry the bacon in a skillet over medium heat for 4 minutes until crispy. Remove and chop. Plate and set aside too.
3. Fetch out 2/3 of the bacon fat and sauté the onions in the remaining grease over medium heat for 2 minutes; set aside. Melt 1 tablespoon of butter in a skillet over medium heat.
4. Lay one tortilla in a skillet; sprinkle with some Swiss cheese. Add some chopped eggs and bacon over the cheese, top with onion, and sprinkle with some cheddar cheese. Cover with another tortilla shell. Cook for 45 seconds, then carefully flip the quesadilla, and cook the

other side too for 45 seconds. Remove to a plate and repeat the cooking process using the remaining tortilla shells.

5. Garnish with parsley and serve warm.

Nutrition:

Kcal 449,

Fat 48.7g,

Net Carbs 6.7g,

Protein 29.1g

12. Chicken Thighs with Vegetables

Preparation Time: 10 Minutes

Cooking Time: 6 Hours

Servings: 6/7

Ingredients:

- 6 chicken thighs
- 1 teaspoon of vegetable oil
- 15 oz. canned tomatoes, diced
- 1 yellow onion, diced
- 2 tablespoon of tomato paste
- 1/2 cup of white wine
- 2 cups of chicken stock
- 1 celery stalk, diced
- 1/4 lb. baby carrots, cut into halves

- 1/2 teaspoon of thyme, dried
- Salt and black pepper- to taste

Directions:

1. Start by throwing all the fixings into the Crockpot and mix them well.
2. Cover it and cook for 6 hours on Low Settings.
3. Shred the slow-cooked chicken using a fork and return to the pot.
4. Mix well and garnish as desired.
5. Serve warm.

Nutrition: Calories 372

Total Fat 11.8 g Saturated Fat 4.4 g

Cholesterol 62 mg Total Carbs 1.8 g

Fiber 0.6 g Sugar 27.3 g Sodium 871 mg Potassium 288 mg

Protein 34 g

13. Chicken Dipped in Tomatillo Sauce

Preparation Time: 10 Minutes

Cooking Time: 7 Hours

Servings: 4

Ingredients:

- 1 lb. chicken thighs, skinless and boneless
- 2 tablespoon of extra virgin olive oil
- 1 yellow onion, sliced
- 1 garlic clove, crushed
- 4 oz. canned green chilies, diced
- 1 handful cilantro, diced
- 15 oz. cauliflower rice, already cooked
- 5 oz. tomatoes, diced
- 15 oz. cheddar cheese, grated

- 4 oz. black olives, pitted and diced
- Salt and black pepper- to taste
- 15 oz canned tomatillos, diced

Directions:

1. Start by throwing all the fixings into the Crockpot and mix them well.
2. Cover it and cook for 5 6 hours on Low Settings.
3. Shred the slow-cooked chicken and return to the pot.
4. Mix well and garnish as desired.
5. Serve warm.

Nutrition:

Calories 427 Total Fat 31.1 g Saturated Fat 4.2 g Cholesterol 0 mg Total Carbs 9 g Sugar 12.4 g Fiber 19.8 g Sodium 86 mg Potassium 100 mg Protein 23.5 g

14. Chicken with Lemon Parsley Butter

Preparation Time: 10 Minutes

Cooking Time: 3 Hours **Servings:** 10

Ingredients:

- 1 (5 – 6lbs) whole roasting chicken, rinsed
- 1 cup of water
- 1/2 teaspoon of kosher salt
- 1/4 teaspoon of black pepper
- 1 whole lemon, sliced
- 4 tablespoons of butter
- 2 tablespoons of fresh parsley, chopped

Directions:

1. Start by seasoning the chicken with all the herbs and spices.

2. Place this chicken in the Crockpot.
3. Cover it and cook for 3 hours on High Settings.
4. Meanwhile, melt butter with lemon slices and parsley in a saucepan.
5. Drizzle the butter over the Crockpot chicken.
6. Serve warm.

Nutrition:

Calories 379 Total Fat 29.7 g

Saturated Fat 18.6 g Cholesterol 141 mg

Total Carbs 9.7g Fiber 0.9 g

Sugar 1.3 g

Sodium 193 mg

Potassium 130 mg

Protein 25.2 g

15. Keto Paprika Chicken

Preparation Time: 10 Minutes

Cooking Time: 8 Hours

Servings: 8

Ingredients:

- 1 free-range whole chicken
- 1 tablespoon of olive oil
- 1 tablespoon of dried paprika
- 1 tablespoon of curry powder
- 1 teaspoon of dried turmeric
- 1 teaspoon of salt

Directions:

1. Start by mixing all the spices and oil in a bowl except chicken.

2. Now season the chicken with these spices liberally.

3. Add the chicken and spices to your Crockpot.

4. Cover the lid of the crockpot and cook for 8 hours on Low.

5. Serve warm.

Nutrition:

Calories 313 Total Fat 134g

Saturated Fat 78 g Cholesterol 861 mg

Total Carbs 6.3 g

Fiber 0.7 g

Sugar 18 g

Sodium 62 mg

Potassium 211 mg

Protein 24.6 g

Dinner

16. Black Bean Salsa

Preparation Time: 10 minutes

Cooking Time: 0 minutes

Servings: 6

Ingredients:

- 1 tablespoon coconut aminos
- ½ teaspoon cumin, ground

- 1 cup canned black beans, no-salt-added, drained and rinsed
- 1 cup salsa
- 6 cups romaine lettuce leaves, torn
- ½ cup avocado, peeled, pitted and cubed

Directions:

- In a bowl, combine the beans with the aminos, cumin, salsa, lettuce and avocado, toss, divide into small bowls and serve as a snack.

Nutrition:

Calories 181

Fat 4 Fiber 7

Carbs 14

Protein 7

17. Mung Sprouts Salsa

Preparation Time: 10 minutes

Cooking Time: 0 minutes

Servings: 2

Ingredients:

- 1 red onion, chopped
- 2 cups Mung beans, sprouted
- A pinch of red chili powder
- 1 green chili pepper, chopped
- 1 tomato, chopped
- 1 teaspoon chaat masala
- 1 teaspoon lemon juice
- 1 tablespoon coriander, chopped
- Black pepper to the taste

Directions:

- In a salad bowl, mix onion with Mung sprouts, chili pepper, tomato, chili powder, chaat masala, lemon juice, coriander and pepper, toss well, divide into small cups and serve.

Nutrition:

Calories 100

Fiber 1

Fat 3

Carbs 3

Protein 6

18. Sprouts and Apples Snack Salad

Preparation Time: 10 minutes

Cooking Time: 0 minutes

Servings: 4

Ingredients:

- 1-pound Brussels sprouts, shredded
- 1 cup walnuts, chopped
- 1 apple, cored and cubed
- 1 red onion, chopped
- For the salad dressing:
- 3 tablespoons red vinegar
- 1 tablespoon mustard
- ½ cup olive oil
- 1 garlic clove, minced

- Black pepper to the taste

Directions:

- In a salad bowl, mix sprouts with apple, onion and walnuts.
- In another bowl, mix vinegar with mustard, oil, garlic and pepper, whisk really well, add this to your salad, toss well and serve as a snack.

Nutrition:

Calories 120

Fat 2

Fiber 2

Carbs 8

Protein 6

19. Dijon Celery Salad

Preparation Time: 10 minutes

Cooking Time: 0 minutes **Servings: 4**

Ingredients:

- 5 teaspoons stevia ½ cup lemon juice
- 1/3 cup Dijon mustard
- 2/3 cup olive oil
- Black pepper to the taste
- 2 apples, cored, peeled and cubed
- 1 bunch celery and leaves, roughly chopped
- ¾ cup walnuts, chopped

Directions:

- In a salad bowl, mix celery and its leaves with apple pieces and walnuts.

- Add black pepper, lemon juice, mustard, stevia and olive oil, whisk well, add to your salad, toss, divide into small cups and serve as a snack.

Nutrition:

Calories 125

Fat 2

Fiber 2

Carbs 7

Protein 7

20. Napa Cabbage Slaw

Preparation Time: 10 minutes

Cooking Time: 0 minutes

Servings: 4

Ingredients:

- ½ cup of red bell pepper, cut into thin strips
- 1 carrot, grated
- 4 cups Napa cabbage, shredded
- 3 green onions, chopped
- 1 tablespoon olive oil
- 2 teaspoons ginger, grated
- ½ teaspoon red pepper flakes, crushed
- 3 tablespoons balsamic vinegar
- 1 tablespoon coconut aminos

- 3 tablespoons low-fat peanut butter

Directions:

- In a salad bowl, mix bell pepper with carrot, cabbage and onions and toss.
- Add oil, ginger, pepper flakes, vinegar, aminos and peanut butter, toss, divide into small cups and serve.

Nutrition:

Calories 160

Fat 10

Fiber 3

Carbs 10

Protein 5

Vegetables

21. Jalapeno and Cheese Egg Muffins

Preparation Time: 10 minutes

Cooking Time: 15 minutes

Servings: 2

Ingredients

- 1 jalapeno pepper, diced
- 2 tbsp. sliced green onions
- 2 tbsp. grated parmesan cheese
- 1 tsp all-purpose seasoning
- 2 eggs
- Seasoning:
- 1/3 tsp salt

- ¼ tsp ground black pepper

Directions:

1. Turn on the oven, then set it to 375 degrees F, and let it preheat.
2. Meanwhile, take two silicone muffin cups, grease with oil, and evenly fill them with cheese, jalapeno pepper, and green onion.
3. Crack eggs in a bowl, season with salt, black pepper, and all-purpose seasoning, whisk well, then evenly pour the mixture into muffin cups and bake for 15 to 20 minutes or until the top is slightly brown and muffins have puffed up.
4. Serve.

Nutrition: 108 Calories; 7.1 g Fats; 8.9 g Protein; 1.8 g Net Carb; 0.4 g Fiber

22. Cheesy Tomato and Olive Muffins

Preparation Time: 10 minutes

Cooking Time: 12 minutes;

Servings: 2

Ingredients

- 4 1/3 tbsp. almond flour
- ½ tbsp. coconut flour
- 1/3 tbsp. chopped tomato
- 1/3 tbsp. sliced green olives
- 2 tbsp. sour cream
- Seasoning:
- 1/8 tsp baking powder
- 2/3 tbsp. avocado oil
- 3 tbsp. grated parmesan cheese

- ½ of egg

Directions:

1. Turn on the oven, then set it to 320 degrees F and let it preheat.
2. Meanwhile, take a medium bowl, place flours in it, and stir in the baking powder until mixed.
3. Add eggs along with sour cream and oil, whisk until blended and then fold in cheese, tomato, and olives until just mixed.
4. Take two silicone muffin cups, add the prepared batter in it evenly and then bake for 10 to 12 minutes until cooked but slightly moist in the middle.
5. When done, let muffin cools for 5 minutes, then take them out and serve.

Nutrition: 256 Calories; 23.5 g Fats; 8.7 g Protein; 1 g Net Carb; 1.8 g Fiber

23. Pumpkin Bread

Preparation Time: 10 minutes

Cooking Time: 25 minutes;

Servings: 2

Ingredients

- 6 tbsp. coconut flour
- 1 tbsp. erythritol sweetener
- ¼ tsp vanilla extract, unsweetened
- 1 egg
- 2 tbsp. pumpkin puree
- Seasoning:
- ¼ tsp baking powder
- ¼ tsp cinnamon
- 1 tbsp. chopped almonds

- 1 ½ tbsp. butter, unsalted, softened

Directions:

1. Turn on the oven, then set it to 350 degrees F and let it preheat.
2. Meanwhile, take a medium bowl, place butter in it, whisk in sugar and egg until fluffy.
3. Add remaining ingredients except for almonds, whisk until incorporated and smooth batter comes together and then fold in almonds until just mixed
4. Take a mini loaf pan, add the prepared batter in it and then bake for 20 to 23 minutes until firm and top have turned nicely browned.
5. When done, let the bread cool for 5 minutes, take out the bread, cut it into slices, and then serve.

Nutrition: 240 Calories; 17.7 g Fats; 9.4 g Protein; 1 g Net Carb; 8.4 g Fiber

24. Buttery Broccoli and Bacon

Preparation Time: 5 minutes;

Cooking Time: 12 minutes;

Servings: 2

Ingredients

1 slice of turkey bacon

1 cup chopped broccoli florets

1/8 tsp garlic powder

¼ tsp Italian seasoning

¼ tbsp. unsalted butter

Seasoning:

1/8 tsp salt

1/8 tsp ground black pepper

Directions:

1. Take a medium skillet pan, place it over high heat, add bacon slice and cook for 3 to 5 minutes until crispy.
2. Transfer bacon to a cutting board and then chop it into small pieces.
3. Reduce the heat to medium-low level, add broccoli florets into the pan, stir well into the bacon grease, add butter, then toss until mixed and cook for 5 minutes until tender.
4. Season the broccoli florets with salt, black pepper, and Italian seasoning, add chopped bacon, stir well and cook for 2 minutes until thoroughly heated.
5. Serve.

Nutrition: 75 Calories; 5 g Fats; 5 g Protein; 1 g Net Carb; 2 g Fiber

25. Broccoli Salad with Bacon

Preparation Time: 5 minutes;

Cooking Time: 0 minutes; **Servings**: 2

Ingredients

- 1 cup broccoli florets, chopped
- 4 tbsp. whipped topping
- 2 tbsp. shredded cheddar cheese
- 3 slices of turkey bacon, cooked, chopped
- 1/3 tsp garlic powder Seasoning: 1/8 tsp salt
- 1/8 tsp dried parsley

Directions:

1. Take a medium bowl, place whipped topping in it, whisk in garlic powder and parsley, and then fold in broccoli florets.

2. Top with bacon and cheddar cheese and serve.

Nutrition: 119 Calories; 10 g Fats; 3.5 g Protein; 2 g Net Carb; 0.5 g Fiber

26. Roasted Green Beans

Preparation Time: 5 minutes

Cooking Time: 25 minutes;

Servings: 2

Ingredients

- ½ pound green beans
- ½ cup grated parmesan cheese
- 3 tbsp. coconut oil
- ½ tsp garlic powder
- Seasoning: 1/3 tsp salt
- 1/8 tsp ground black pepper

Directions:

1. Turn on the oven, then set it to 425 degrees F, and let preheat.

2. Take a baking sheet, line green beans on it, and set aside until required.
3. Prepare the dressing, and for this, place remaining ingredients in a bowl, except for cheese and whisk until combined.
4. Drizzle the dressing over green beans, toss until well coated, and then bake for 20 minutes until green beans are tender-crisp.
5. Then sprinkle cheese on top of beans and continue roasting for 3 to 5 minutes or until cheese melts and nicely golden brown.
6. Serve.

Nutrition: 119 Calories; 9 g Fats; 5 g Protein; 4.5 g Net Carb; 3 g Fiber

Meat

27. Beef, Pepper and Green Beans Stir-fry

Preparation Time: 5 minutes;

Cooking Time: 18 minutes

Servings: 2

Ingredients

- 6 oz. ground beef
- 2 oz. chopped green bell pepper
- 4 oz. green beans
- 3 tbsp. grated cheddar cheese

- Seasoning:
- ½ tsp salt
- ¼ tsp ground black pepper
- ¼ tsp paprika

Directions:

1. Take a skillet pan, place it over medium heat, add ground beef and cook for 4 minutes until slightly browned.
2. Then add bell pepper and green beans, season with salt, paprika, and black pepper, stir well and continue cooking for 7 to 10 minutes until beef and vegetables have cooked through.
3. Sprinkle cheddar cheese on top, then transfer pan under the broiler and cook for 2 minutes until cheese has melted and the top is golden brown.

4. Serve.

Nutrition: 282.5 Calories; 17.6 g Fats; 26.1 g Protein; 2.9 g Net Carb; 2.1 g Fiber;

28. Cheesy Meatloaf

Preparation Time: 5 minutes

Cooking Time: 4 minutes

Servings: 2

Ingredients

- 4 oz. ground turkey
- 1 egg 1 tbsp. grated mozzarella cheese
- ¼ tsp Italian seasoning
- ½ tbsp. soy sauce
- Seasoning: ¼ tsp salt
- 1/8 tsp ground black pepper

Directions:

1. Take a bowl, place all the ingredients in it, and stir until mixed.

2. Take a heatproof mug, spoon in prepared mixture and microwave for 3 minutes at high heat setting until cooked.
3. When done, let meatloaf rest in the mug for 1 minute, then take it out, cut it into two slices and serve.

Nutrition: 196.5 Calories; 13.5 g Fats; 18.7 g Protein; 18.7 g Net Carb; 0 g Fiber;

Poultry and Eggs

29. Chili Chicken Kabobs with Tahini

Preparation Time: 20 Minutes+ 2 Hours Refrigeration

Cooking Time: 10 Minutes

Servings: 6

Ingredients

- 3 tbsp. soy sauce
- 1 tbsp. ginger-garlic paste
- 2 tbsp. swerve brown sugar

- 2 tbsp. olive oil
- 3 chicken breasts, cut into bite-sized cubes
- ½ cup tahini
- ½ tsp garlic powder
- Salt and chili pepper to taste

Directions

1. In a bowl, whisk soy sauce, ginger-garlic paste, swerve brown sugar, chili pepper, and olive oil. Put the chicken in a zipper bag, pour the marinade over, seal, and shake for an even coat. Marinate in the fridge for 2 hours.
2. Preheat a grill to 400 F and thread the chicken on skewers. Cook for 10 minutes in total with three to four turnings to be golden brown. Plate them.

3. Mix the tahini, garlic powder, salt, and ¼ cup of warm water in a bowl. Serve the chicken skewers and tahini dressing with cauliflower fried rice.

Nutrition Calories 225, Net Carbs 2g, Fat 17.4g, Protein 15g

30. Chicken with Eggplant & Tomatoes

Preparation Time: 25 Minutes

Cooking Time: 10 Minutes

Servings: 4

Ingredients

- 2 tbsp. ghee 1 lb. chicken thighs
- Salt and black pepper to taste
- 2 cloves garlic, minced
- 1 (14 oz.) can whole tomatoes
- 1 eggplant, diced
- 10 fresh basil leaves, chopped + extra to garnish

Directions

1. Melt ghee in a saucepan over medium heat, season the chicken with salt and black pepper, and fry for 4 minutes

on each side until golden brown. Remove the chicken onto a plate.

2. Sauté the garlic in the ghee for 2 minutes, pour in the tomatoes, and cook covered for 8 minutes. Include the eggplant and basil. Cook for 4 minutes.
3. Season the sauce with salt and black pepper, stir and add the chicken. Coat with sauce and simmer for 3 minutes.
4. Serve chicken with sauce on a bed of squash pasta garnished with basil.

Nutrition Calories 465, Net Carbs 2g, Fat 39.5g, Protein 26g

Seafood

31. Cheesy Garlic Bread with Salmon

Preparation Time: 10 minutes

Cooking Time: 1 minute;

Servings: 2

Ingredients

- 4 tbsp. almond flour
- ½ tsp baking powder
- 2 tbsp. grated cheddar cheese
- 1 egg
- 2 oz. salmon, cut into thin sliced
- Seasoning:
- 1 tbsp. butter, unsalted

- ¼ tsp garlic powder
- 1/8 tsp salt
- ¼ tsp Italian seasoning

Directions:

1. Take a heatproof bowl, place all the ingredients in it except for cheese and then stir by using a fork until well combined.
2. Fold in cheese until just mixed and then microwave for 1 minute at high heat setting until thoroughly cooked, else continue cooking for another 15 to 30 seconds.
3. When done, lift out the bread, cool it for 5 minutes and then cut it into slices.
4. Top each slice with salmon and then serve straight away

Nutrition: 233 Calories; 18 g Fats; 13.8 g Protein; 1.9 g Net Carb; 1.5 g Fiber

32. Salmon Pasta Salad

Preparation Time: 10 minutes

Cooking Time: 0 minutes;

Servings: 2

Ingredients

- 1 zucchini, spiralized into noodles
- 4 oz. smoked salmon, break into pieces
- 2 oz. cream cheese
- 2 oz. mayonnaise
- 2 oz. sour cream
- Seasoning:
- 1/3 tsp salt
- ¼ tsp ground black pepper
- ¼ tsp hot sauce

Directions:

1. Take a medium bowl, place cream cheese in it, add mayonnaise, sour cream, salt, black pepper and hot sauce and stir until well combined.
2. Add zucchini noodles, toss until well coated and then fold in salmon until just mixed.
3. Serve.

Nutrition: 458 Calories; 38.7 g Fats; 15.4 g Protein; 6.1 g Net Carb; 1.7 g Fiber

Snacks

33. nds

Preparation Time: 10 minutes

Cooking Time: 10 minutes

Servings 12

Ingredients:

- Bacon, cooked and chopped – 12 ounces
- Chopped sweet red pepper – 2 tablespoons
- Medium white onion, peeled and chopped – 1
- Salt – 3/4 teaspoon
- Ground black pepper – 1/2 teaspoon
- Almonds, chopped – 1/2 cup
- Cheddar cheese, grated – 1 pound

- Avocado mayonnaise – 2 cups

Directions:

1. Place all the ingredients for the dip in a medium bowl and stir until combined.
2. Divide dip evenly between small bowls and serve as a party dip.

Nutrition: calories: 184, fat: 12, fiber: 1, carbs: 4, protein: 5

34. Green Tabasco Devilled Eggs

Preparation Time: 20 minutes

Cooking Time: 10 minutes

Servings: 6

Ingredients:

- 6 Eggs
- 1/3 cup Mayonnaise
- 1 ½ tbsp. Green Tabasco
- Salt and Pepper, to taste

Directions:

1. Place the eggs in a saucepan over medium heat and pour boiling water over, enough to cover them.
2. Cook for 6-8 minutes.
3. Place in an ice bath to cool.

4. When safe to handle, peel the eggs and slice them in half.
5. Scoop out the yolks and place in a bowl.
6. Add the remaining ingredients.
7. Whisk to combine.
8. Fill the egg holes with the mixture.
9. Serve and enjoy!

Nutrition:

Calories 175

Total Fats 17g

Net Carbs: 5g

Protein 6g

Fiber: 1g

Salads

35. Seared Squid Salad with Red Chili Dressing

Preparation Time: 10 Minutes

Cooking Time: 5 Minutes

Servings: 4

Ingredients:

- 4 medium squid tubes, cut into rings
- 1 tablespoon chopped cilantro, for garnish

Salad:

- 1 cup arugula
- 2 medium cucumbers, halved and cut in strips
- ½ red onion, finely sliced
- ½ cup mint leaves
- ½ cup cilantro leaves, reserve the stems
- Salt and black pepper, to taste
- 2 tablespoons olive oil, divided

Direction:

1. Make the salad: Mix the arugula, cucumber strips, red onion, mint leaves, and coriander leaves in a salad bowl. Add the salt, pepper, and 1 tablespoon olive oil. Toss to combine well and set aside.

2. Make the dressing: Lightly pound the red chili, garlic clove, and Swerve in a clay mortar with a wooden pestle until it forms a coarse paste. Mix in the lime juice and fish sauce. Set aside.
3. Warm the remaining olive oil in a skillet over high heat. Add the squid and sear for about 5 minutes until lightly browned.
4. Transfer the squid to the salad bowl and top with the dressing. Stir well. Serve garnished with the cilantro.

Nutrition:

Calories: 278 Cal Fat: 24 g

Carbs: 6 g

Protein: 7 g

Fiber: 5 g

Soups and Stews

36. Sausage Soup with Tomatoes & Zucchini Noodles

Preparation time: 30 minutes

Cook Time: 1 ¾ hours

Servings: 8

Ingredients:

- Turkey/pork Italian sausage (19.5 oz. pkg.)
- Olive oil (1 tbsp.)
- Chicken stock (8 cups from a carton/can/homemade)

- Tomato paste (2 tbsp.)
- Petite tomatoes - diced (2 cans/14.5 oz. each)
- Dried basil (1 tbsp.)
- Dried Greek oregano (2 tsp.)
- Optional: Ground fennel (2 tsp.)
- Green and red bell peppers (half of each one)
- Onion (half of one medium)
- Medium zucchini (2 @10-inches long)
- Black pepper & salt (as desired)

Direction:

1. Chop the onions and peppers.
2. Heat a skillet with a bit of oil and add the sausage to cook until it's browned thoroughly.
3. Combine the sausage, tomato paste, diced tomatoes, chicken stock, and spices into the soup pot. Wait for

it to simmer.

4. Dice the bell peppers and onion. Sauté them for a few minutes and toss them into the soup. Simmer them using the low-temperature setting (30-60 min.).

5. Prepare the zucchini into noodles using a veggie peeler or spiralizer. Add them to the soup and simmer on low (20-30 min.).

6. Serve them hot, with a portion of freshly grated parmesan as desired

Nutrition:

Calories: 497

Net Carbohydrates: 4 g

Protein: 55 g

Fat Content: 27 g

37. Shirataki Soup

Preparation time: 10 minutes

Cook Time: 20 minutes

Servings: 2

Ingredients:

- Boneless - skinless chicken thighs (2)
- Chicken stock (3 cups)
- Minced ginger (1 tsp.)
- Cardamom (.25 tsp.)
- Minced garlic (1 clove)
- Mushrooms (.5 cup)
- Optional: Chili sauce (1 tsp.)
- Chopped cilantro (1 pinch)
- Thinly sliced chili pepper (1)

Directions:

1. Heat the stock on the stovetop using the med-high temperature setting. Toss in the ginger, garlic, mushrooms, and cardamom. Simmer for about ten minutes.
2. Fold in the chicken and cook until done or about five minutes.
3. Prepare two soup bowls and add the sliced chili pepper to each dish. Serve the soup and garnish with some cilantro.
4. Adjust spices as desired.

Nutrition:

Calories: 130 Net Carbohydrates: 1.5 g

Protein: 29.4 g Fat Content: 10 g

DESSERTS

38. Heart Chocolates

Preparation: 20 min ready in 2 h 20 min

Ingredients

- 100 g whole milk coverture
- 100 g dark chocolate coverture
- 100 g coconut oil
- 125 ml whipped cream at least 30% fat content
- 50 g nut nougat cream

Preparation steps

1. Cut the two types of coverture and the coconut oil into small pieces. Heat the cream with the coverture, the nut nougat cream, and the coconut oil in a saucepan and melt everything over a medium heat while stirring.

2. Let the mixture cool down a little. Pour the chocolate cream into the molds up to approx. 1 mm below the edge and allow solidifying in the refrigerator.

39. Caramel Candies (2nd Version)

Preparation: 25 min ready in 40 min

Ingredients

- 200 g sugar
- 150 g honey
- 1 organic orange zest
- 250 ml whipped cream at least 30% fat content
- 50 g butter

Preparation steps

1. Put the sugar, honey, and 5 tablespoons of water in a saucepan and let it simmer for 2-3 minutes. Add the orange peel. Pour the cream into a large saucepan and

bring to the boil. Pour in the caramel sugar and cook for about 10 minutes while stirring.

2. As a test, let a few drops of caramel mass drip onto a cool plate or marble board. If the mass becomes firm, it is okay. Stir in the butter. Line a rectangular candy mold (approx. 20x30 cm) with aluminum foil, oil it, pour in the mixture, and allow to cool.

3. Then fall onto a large board and peel off the foil. Divide into candy with an oiled knife. Then let the caramel candies cool down completely.

40. Toffees with Mocha

Preparation: 30 min ready in 6 h 30 min

Ingredients

- 200 ml whipped cream at least 30% fat content
- 2 tbsp instant mocha
- 200 ml caramel syrup
- 200 g sugar

Preparation steps

1. Bring the cream with the mocha to the boil in a saucepan, remove from the heat, draw and let cool completely.

2. Strain the cream through a fine sieve and bring it to the boil together with the syrup and sugar while stirring and let simmer for about 10-15. Remove from the heat, place in a tin lined with aluminum foil, spread smoothly, and let cool down.

3. Cut the toffee into cubes and serve.

CPSIA information can be obtained
at www.ICGtesting.com
Printed in the USA
BVHW010359260621
610374BV00003B/139

9 781914 387357